Naked Sayulita 2016

Contents

1. The Airport
2. Transportation
3. Accommodations
4. Police
5. Drinking
6. Eating
7. Prostitution
8. Crime
9. The Beaches
10. Surfing and SUP
11. Nightlife
12. Medical
13. Drugs
14. Jail
15. Sports
16. Vendors
17. Dogs
18. Internet, Cell Phones and Mail
19. Locals and the Mayor
20. Side Trips
21. Bikes, Boats and ATVs
22. Festivals and Holidays
23. Donating and Volunteering

Intro

Sayulita is a small, beach town located about 45 minutes north of Puerto Vallarta. Although home of the 2012 movie, 'Beverly Hills Chihuahua', this isn't the happiest place on earth, so understand that right now. People have been murdered, robbed, raped and more here; I know, I have lived here full time for over 10 years.

This guide contains the meat and potatoes of things that make Sayulita and is for people who want straight-up, unbiased information. No one has 'contributed' one peso to the creation of this guide, nor is anyone telling me what to put in it or what not to.

Ever wonder why certain websites only have positive reviews of places to stay on them? Just put two and two together and it's not because no one has ever complained.

"Why isn't this anywhere else?" The answer is because many do not want to jeopardize their profits. This guide contains stories verified to be true and no names have been mentioned.

Sayulita is completely different than anywhere in Mexico and at times feels like the old west. This is not like home. It is not going to change, so don't waste your time trying.

Instead of writing 200-300 pages of unnecessary crap just to fill up space, I have edited this down so you are only getting what is necessary.

The Airport

The nearest airport is PVR, or Puerto Vallarta. If you are **arriving**, after disembarking, you will go through immigration, where they will give you a paper good for anywhere from 90 to 180 days. Do not lose this, as you cannot fly out without it!

After clearing immigration, continue on through customs. Here you put your luggage through a scanner and will push a button and receive either a red or a green light. If you get the green light, proceed through what we call the 'gauntlet'. If you draw the red light, you will need to be checked through a secondary inspection.

Once you are done in immigration, just one more step until you are out. Unfortunately, this step is annoying as hell. I always throw on my sunglasses at this point and walk straight ahead.

After you make it through the sliding doors of customs, you will be greeted by two rows of people trying to get you into some type of timeshare or other promotion. They will tell you almost anything to get your attention. My best advice is to completely ignore them and walk quickly through to the meet and greet area.

You will see a cluster of people waiting on the outside of the area. If you are expecting someone, they will be here. There are women in booths that can get you a taxi if you would like before exiting the area and out into the public.

There are restrooms to your right, once you leave the area and into the general population of the airport. If you want a drink, there is a small 4 table bar located just outside the restroom. The drinks are a little pricey, but it's in the airport.

Once you leave the comfort of the airport, the humidity will hit you immediately once you exit. There is an OXXO here (like a 7-eleven) and you can get a snack, beer or whatever here. The inside is air-conditioned and they have covered tables where you will see a variety of people on their break from work, travelers departing or simply waiting. This area is usually congested, but safe.

If you are **departing**, there is an OXXO when you arrive at the airport, if you would like to save some money. Once you get inside the airport, you will see agents for your airline. Make sure to have the 'tourist visa' they gave you when you came in. If you don't, you will need to go to the immigration office there and pay a fine.

When you have your ticket, take the escalator up to the second level. You will find a Carl's junior if you're hungry and they even serve beer.

Continuing along, there is a board with the airlines departing on your right side. You can choose from a variety of eateries and drinking spots before security. There is one, which has basic food and a full bar with TV's. This is ideal if you are with someone who is not travelling with you.

One you reach the security checkpoint, have your passport ready and remove your belt. Basic rules apply here. Security is usually pretty quick and should not take more than 10 minutes.

Past security, walk past the moving sidewalks, that never move and through the duty free shopping. There are two main, full service restaurants inside. First is one that has a bar and seating, with TV's and a departure display. This spot is pretty relaxing and close to your gate.

A recent addition to the airport is Bubba Gumps Shrimp Company, a fun place to hang out before taking off and my personal favorite inside security.

If you are not familiar with it, it is pretty cute if you have young people or if you like the movie, 'Forrest Gump.' This has everything the other Bubba Gumps have as far as food and drinks available.

This is also the last, full-service restaurant before you head to your departure gate. It is actually close enough to most where you can hear announcements.

All of these offer many solid food-to-go options, so you are able to take something on the plane to snack on. They have a legitimate jewelry place next to the gates that sells a variety of real silver and prices are based on weight.

Transportation

From the airport:

There are two main ways to get to Sayulita from the airport. The first is a **taxi**. Once you exit the airport you will be approached by dozens of people offering you a taxi. The reality is they are all fairly equal, so if you just want to get to Sayulita, take your pick.

There are a variety of vehicles that can accommodate up to 8 people. The rates are pretty standard and will run about 500 to 1000 pesos for a one way trip.

If you want to stop and do some grocery shopping, all taxis can stop at either Wal-Mart in Nuevo Vallarta or Mega in Bucerias. Before committing, ask your driver the total cost with shopping included. Most taxis have this in the rate, just check to make sure.

The taxi drivers are very territorial. I mention this because last year I met a couple who liked their driver so much, they wanted him to pick them up to go back to the airport. Before he could pick them up, other local cab drivers were threatening and blocked him from picking up his clients.

My personal favorite is a driver by the name of Fabian, who runs Sayulita Transportation. He is licensed to both pick-up and drop-off clients at the airport. He also has air-conditioning and a cooler that is always stocked with ice cold beer and water. He has no idea he is mentioned here.

A more economical option is the taking the local **bus**. The cost is a mere 30 pesos for the ride to Sayulita and you can carry on and enjoy your food and drinks with the locals. It makes frequent stops, but is safe and will take about an hour.

To find the bus going to Sayulita, once you exit the airport, make a left towards the main highway. You will see an overhead walkway connecting the north and southbound lanes.

Walk up the ramp and over the freeway. There is usually a frail older woman who sits here and politely asks for spare change. Walk over and down to the other side.

You will see many busses pulling up and people getting on and off, notice where they are standing. Around are economically friendly places to get some food or drinks.

The bus going to Sayulita will have a sign in the front window, either across the top, or in the corner. It will have many destinations listed, but Sayulita and Vallarta are the two that are listed first and last on the route.

Some of the busses **you do not want** to get on are:

- Punta de Mita
- Valle Dorado
- Bucerias
- Nuevo Vallarta
- San Vicente

Your bus will have both Bucerias and Mezcales listed on the route, just make sure that the bus you're getting on reads **Sayulita**. The buses that have San Pancho or Los de Marcos listed will also make a stop in Sayulita. These do not run often, but are an option.

The schedule for the bus to Sayulita is every 20 minutes. If you are taking it from Sayulita, they will depart 20 minutes past the hour and every 20 minutes thereafter.

In Town:

The most popular type of transportation aside from car or taxi is a **golf car**. Most of Sayulita can be accessed with one of these and they are easy to drive. There are two types currently available in town, an electric and a gas car.

An electric golf car requires it to be charged, usually overnight. A problem with the electric cars is that the charger is very expensive, so make sure you have a secure place to hook it up, before committing to one.

A gas powered car has a bit more power and there is a Pemex gas station at the entrance to town to fill it up.

The two main companies in town are Sayulita Golf Cars and Town Around. Both of them are solid choices and accept credit cards.

Renting a car is an option as well. There is one office located across from the 'Drunk Tree' downtown. This is a large tree in the center of the 'Y' when you go over the bridge and into town. You will see locals mingling on the stone bench and occasionally vendors selling fresh-cut flowers.

Accommodations

When selecting a place to stay, there are a few types of accommodations. They include:

- Hotels
- Resorts and Bungalows
- Private Homes
- Hostels

Hotels

Hotels make up a growing market when it comes to lodging in Sayulita. A huge benefit to staying in a hotel is security. Property crime is very high in town, so being in a hotel with 24 hour security can be a big relief.

A hotel is self-explanatory and you will find a small variety to choose from. You will not find the all-inclusive giants that you do in Nuevo or P.V however.

Hotel Diamante is located on the north end and is the oldest in town. It is a secure, well maintained, no-frills option and just a block from the beach. This also has a pool and under a dozen rooms that can be rented by the day, week or month.

Condos and Bungalows

These make up a nice niche in Sayulita. Generally speaking, bungalows are several semi-private structures in a location.

Bungalows are safe for the most part and usually have some type of security in place. They are also a bit more economical, than a private home.

A few solid choices include:

- Sayulita Trailer Park and Bungalows: These are simple, comfortable, and quiet. They also are all within a hundred yards of the beach on the north end.

- <u>Junto el Rio</u>: Classic style wooden bungalows that are safe and steps from the north end beach. The river is next door so the occasional smell of sewage can be unpleasant.
- <u>Villa Amor</u>: Located on the far south end, this is the jewel of Sayulita bungalows. Branded as a resort, it has many multi-bedroom bungalows available on the hill and all have ocean views. This is very safe, quiet and has a brand new spa on the grounds.

Condos

Condos make up a small part of the vacation rental market in town, but highly regarded for safety, location and comfort. They are individually owned and usually have 2-3 bedrooms.

Located on the north end of town are a few choices:

- <u>Los Delphines:</u> This small complex has 2 community pools and the grounds are well maintained. Located right on the beach and safe.

Private Homes

Private homes make up the majority of the vacation rental market in Sayulita. What I will say about these is please make sure you have some type of security. Many owners live elsewhere and have a 'manager' to take care of the property.

Property crimes are very high in town. With people staying in private homes, they are automatically targets for theft. No one wants to hear this, but it is true.

You won't hear about this, because certain popular websites refuse to allow people to post negative reviews of properties they promote. If a negative review is posted, it is immediately removed from the site. The owners pay an annual fee, so you will just see positive comments.

'A family had a wedding reception at a private home in Sayulita that was rented for the weekend. The first night, they all went to dinner in town. A couple of hours later some returned to find their belongings strewn around and many personal items missing. This included cell *phones and personal laptops. They were only away from the house for a couple of hours!'*

Hostals

Hostals in the past few years have sprung up in Sayulita, as an affordable option. With rates around $200 pesos ($12.00) per night, if you just want a place to stay and aren't picky, these are for you.

Hostal Sayulita is located in the Tamarindo area, close to the center of town.

Hostal Lolita is just off the main road into town, on the north end.

Both of these are around a 5 minute walk to the town plaza and the beach. Really no frills and price driven, you get what you pay for.

Police

Police and law enforcement are broken into four specific categories. Unlike their counterparts up north, each has a specific jurisdiction and is limited in what they can do.

Transito

Transito are responsible for traffic and parking enforcement. In Sauylita traffic is a becoming huge problem and finding a parking place is similar to locating one at Fisherman's Wharf, San Francisco.

Those cars that are parked illegally in town may be towed or cited. If a car is ticketed, the Transito will remove the license plates. In order to get your plates back, you need to go to the station in Mezcales and pay the fine.

They do not carry guns and cannot arrest anyone. In fact, if someone is pulled over and it is determined that there has been a criminal offense committed, Transito will need to contact another agency to actually make the arrest. If you get a fine for speeding, they take your license. You will get it back when you pay it.

Transito is also limited in information access. For example, if you have an outstanding ticket in Jalisco state (Puerto Vallarta), Nayarit will not have a clue.

Policia Municipal

The name stands for county police. This group is responsible for the general enforcement of the laws. They react to general disturbances, fights and other matters requiring a police presence.

They are responsible for arresting and transporting people to jail. Policia Municipal carry automatic weapons and handguns. Although intimidating at first sight, they are usually rather friendly and will help you if needed. Please note that English is not usually spoken, so a decent handle on the Spanish language will go far when interacting with the police.

A reality is that the Policia Municipal have to purchase their own guns, uniforms and general items to do their job. There was a Commandante who had a young partner. This partner couldn't afford a weapon, so while he was on duty, the Commandante let him borrow one of his.

Their jurisdiction is Bahia de Banderas, from Nuevo Vallarta to San Pancho and work 24 hour shifts, with 24 on and 24 off. Officers are relocated often to avoid corruption.

Policia Estatal

These are the State Police of Nayarit. They have very similar responsibilities as the Local Police and you will also see them around Sayulita.

The main difference is they work for the state, which makes no difference to a citizen. They also make up the 'Tourist Police', with the only police office located at the beginning of town, next to the veterinarian.

Driving white SUVs', with the colors of Nayarit, the Tourist Police come off as less intimidating than their local counterparts. Something that both the state and local police have in common is that just as Transito can't arrest someone, these cannot pull anyone over for a traffic violation.

Policia Federal

The Federales are the top of the police food chain. They have basically unlimited power. They can pull someone over and arrest them and their resources are unmatched in Mexico.

They are very professional looking and with that can be intimidating. This is the most respected of the agencies by Mexican people.

Bribes vs Fines or Arrest

The term bribe is an ugly one, but the reality is if you are faced with going to jail or paying a bribe, most will choose the latter. It is not an option up north, as this is a black and white issue. In Mexico there is a gray area and you at least have an option most of the time.

Driving from Sayulita to Punta de Mita, a man was pulled over on a motorcycle. He didn't wear a helmet, didn't have a motorcycle license and the motorcycle's tags had expired.

Transito explained the violations and how that if they wanted could impound the bike. They also expressed that $500 pesos would take care of it for the time being. What would you do?

Drinking

General Attitude

Drinking in public is generally tolerated in Sayulita but against the law. You can go to most big cities in Mexico and find the open container law enforced. Sayulita is different and traveling to other areas, I have often heard people saying, "You can't do that, this is not Sayulita."

There was an incident with a couple of North American tourists who happened to be drinking across from a liquor establishment. The police rolled up on them and demanded $500 pesos, as it is technically illegal and they got it.

Aside from that particular incident, I have never heard of anyone being cited or shaken down due to drinking in public. You will see loads of people walking the streets of town with open containers.

Hours of Sales

The exact hours can change depending on the time of season and Holidays. Generally, bars and restaurants have liquor available until two in the morning.

Liquor stores and OXXO sell liquor between 9am and 9pm. Something that is worth noting, is that no liquor is sold on **election** weekend. This law applies not only to the Mexican people, but to everyone.

There was a large wedding party who decided to have their event in Sayulita one weekend. Unfortunately, that particular weekend happened to coincide with the state elections. They were sadly surprised to say the least when they couldn't find liquor for sale _anywhere_ in town.

This holds true for the entire state of Nayarit and shockingly no exceptions apply. One option is to cross into Jalisco state if you are unfortunately in town during elections. Puerto Vallarta happens to be located in Jalisco. If you come to Sayulita during the Presidential elections you're just fucked.

Drinking and Driving

Drinking and driving is illegal in Mexico and that shouldn't come as a surprise to anyone. Although this is certainly not enforced to the extreme as up north, good advice is not to risk it. The Federales have recently added high-quality breathalyzers to their arsenal, so be aware this no longer something law enforcement takes lightly.

A local teacher was intoxicated after a day of drinking and drove north to the capital of Tepic. Once there he was stopped by the Federales. They arrested him and impounded his car. The next day, he was required to pay a $10,000 pesos fine and the fees for the impound lot. This however, did not go on his permanent record.

A brilliant way to recycle is in effect in Mexico. If you purchase a bottle of Pacifico or Corona beer, you will pay a **deposit** of about 30-40 percent. When you return the bottle, you get your deposit back, or just keep turning one in to get another.

Eating

Types of Food Available

Sayulita has the most diverse restaurants this side of Vallarta. You will find authentic Mexican, Italian, up-scale American and many others. Restaurants on the whole, have a huge turnover here, yet once one closes, another is right there to take its place.

Just because a restaurant in another area is successful does not mean it will be successful in Sayulita. Some examples of successful restaurants failing in town are, The Cuban Bar and Fajita Banana. Amazingly at this point, with so many different types of cuisines available, not one Chinese food restaurant exists in town.

Seafood is very popular and you can get fresh fish or shrimp anytime of the year. As many restaurants serve it, there are two that truly stand out:

El Coleguita: Originally in Vallarta and always crowded, Coleguita arrived in Sayulita last year. Their menu is all seafood and lots of it. Free tequila, soup, caramelized bananas and coffee liquor to help with digestion, accompany all entrees. This is located just down from the OXXO at the crucero leading into town.

El Costenos: Located right on the beach, this was one of the very first restaurants in Sayulita. It is no frills and service can be a little slow, but all fish and shrimp entrees are $120 pesos. Beers are the lowest price on the beach at $20 pesos and the margaritas are the strongest in town.

Upscale Dining

There are many places that pop up every year in town, however two have been in Sayulita consistently for over a decade and both are 'vendor free'.

Don Pedros: This is at the top of the list when it comes to up-scale dining. Located right on the beach, the consistency of the quality of service, food and ambience is un-matched. It is expensive compared to other places, hence the local term, 'Don Pay-More.'

Calypsos: Located right on the Plaza, the upper level gives a great view for the special events going on. Open for dinner, this has a full bar, solid selection of entrees and comfortable seating, all overlooking the plaza.

Food Trucks

During your time in Sayulita you will hear trucks with loudspeakers slowly driving along. Unless you are fluent in Spanish, you may just dismiss it as noise.

Listen for key words they say, "*Camaron Fresco, Pollo Fresco, Tamales, Platano, etc...*" The trucks drive slowly and you just need to get their attention for them to stop. This is advertising Fresh Shrimp, Chicken, Tamales and Bananas.

The shrimp and fish trucks have an open truck bed with 2-3 coolers and a scale. I have never experienced spoiled seafood from the trucks. You can get a kilo of medium-large shrimp with the head for $100 pesos ($7.00). The fish is about the same price and is conveniently filleted.

Vegetable trucks cruise around and I recently saw one selling avocados at 3 kilos for $10 pesos. Great deal if you like guacamole. A variety of vegetables can be purchased off the trucks, including potatoes, apples, peppers, tomatoes and onions.

Carnicerias or butcher shops are great for items if you want to cook or barbecue at your home. The best one specifically caters to North-Americans and is located to the right of the 'drunk tree'. Depending on the season, you can get solid cuts of rib eye, t-bone and New York steaks.

Fresh chicken, ribs, flank steak and pork are usually available. They also carry a variety of spices, marinades and sauces. For those that want cheese-its, this is the place. It will cost you about $75 pesos, but surprisingly you won't find them anywhere else.

Prostitution

Prostitution is legal in Mexico, however 'pimping' is not. That is something that people do not quite understand. Promoting prostitution is illegal.

In Sayulita, there are places that cater to locals and serve little beers called **Cantinas**. Here they employ women from other parts of the country as waitresses.

A beer in one of these is around 15 pesos, but the women will encourage you to buy them a beer and this will be double or triple in price. Some of the women are available for sex, but it depends on the woman. If you are wondering, just ask them.

The rates to take a lady out are generally $500-$1000 pesos, depending. Ladies usually work a contact for a few weeks and then go back home after. The cantinas are open from around 10 in the morning until 10 in the evening daily.

A former Sayulita Real Estate broker went to a cantina and picked up one of the ladies. As he was married, he didn't want to bring her home, so he grabbed the keys to one of his listings and partied the night away in there.

Vallarta

Puerto Vallarta has many different areas and places where prostitution is available. From the variety of upscale gentlemen's clubs and cantinas, to the ladies who walk the street, you can find many different options.

One solid option is the renewed, '**Red Zone Tours**.' This company gives tours of the different cantinas that encourage prostitution. The rate is $100 US and includes your first drink, not the women.

Old Town after 6pm begins to have some women walking the streets looking to make some money. The cheap hotels in the area run around 200 pesos and are definitely no frills. Please be very aware when picking up any prostitute that it is not regulated and you won't get much sympathy if something goes foul.

Gentlemen's Clubs are almost all up-scale and offer lap dancing across the board. Most of the time a dancer is available to be taken out for a fee payable to the club, in addition to her own. Be aware that these are pricey and you can expect to drop a few thousand pesos, even before getting a woman to a hotel.

The bigger cities of Mexico have what in essence are **Sex Hotels**. These are rented every 8 hours of so. You drive in, usually through an electronic gate and park in a designated spot.

In the room there is porn on TV, a shower and a bed. A menu of alcoholic beverages is located on the wall and you can call and order what you want. It will arrive in a type of dumb-waiter. You never actually see the people who work there and you will send the money for the room through the dumb-waiter as well.

If you take a taxi, you can either ask them to wait or come back at a designated time. Either way you will pay, so don't pinch pennies at this point.

Crime

Sayulita has received an incredible amount of publicity, drawing to it tourists from all over the world. This unfortunately isn't the only thing it attracts. Criminals from all over come to Sayulita to take advantage of the incredible influx of tourism.

Violent crime is few and far between in town. Limited to basically after hour bar fights on occasion, people are generally safe to walk the streets at night. This doesn't mean forget your common sense. Even in the happiest place on earth shit happens every once in awhile.

One day, a young girl and her parents approached someone in Sayulita. The girl was crying and the parents explained that a man exposed himself to her and is always looming around their property. The little girl is frightened and is scared to go outside now.

A call was made to the local police commandante who responded within 10 minutes. He explained that they have been trying to get this man, but every time they get close he takes off running.

A random meeting took place and a group of six people from Sayulita, including the police descended upon the plaza where he was sleeping. When awakened he began attacking officers and tried running, but was cut off and tackled. After a brief scuffle he was put in the back of the police truck and handcuffed to the roll bar. He was subsequently arrested and never seen after that day in Sayulita.

Herm Edwards, a formal NFL player and coach has something called the 12 o'clock rule. He says that nothing good happens after 12 o' clock and he is right. If you are involved in a fight and police are called, more than likely you will be taken to jail* for a short period and given a fine.

The way the system works in Mexico, is that if you have a complaint that is criminal in nature, then you need to go to Bucerias and fill out a report with the 'Ministerio Publico.

This office does not speak English, so it is recommended to speak to a lawyer to help with the process. There used to be a liaison with a group in Sayulita called 'Neighbor's Watching', who would go with a person who experienced a property crime. They would in turn translate all the necessary paperwork and submit it to the Ministerio Publico.

Once they receive a valid complaint, they will alert the police to take appropriate action. Someone who can be a huge resource if you need to file a report or if you are arrested for a crime is a Mexican lawyer. Her name is Lydia Garcia and she speaks fluent English and Spanish. Her phone number is 322-109-7835. She can also be contacted via email at lgslawyer@hotmail.com.

*See the section on Jail.

The Beaches

There are three beaches in Sayulita. The main beach, the north end beach and Los Muertos beach. They have a life of their own with vendors, surf stands, massage tables and lounge chairs.

Hidden Threats

Something that most people aren't aware of are the **sting-rays** that hide beneath the surface of the shallow shore break. They bury themselves under the sand and if you step on them, will sting. The pain is excruciating, though not life-threatening.

A helpful tip to avoid the rays is to shuffle your feet in the sand when entering the water. This will disturb them and cause them to move elsewhere. If you are stung, go immediately to the pharmacy for relief.

The ocean is unpredictable and in Sayulita, don't let the calm sea fool you. The **undertow** can be brutal. A person drowning is a reality and there are sometimes flags in front of La Terrazolas and Captain Pablo's restaurants that give the current water conditions.

Main Beach

This is the heartbeat of Sayulita. It spans from the river to the creek next to Don Pedro's restaurant. The establishments that line the beach have umbrellas and chairs set up on the beach daily. It is recommended to go early to get a spot.

The **vendors** are and have always been a part of Sayulita. They walk up and down the beach selling a variety of items including, blankets, umbrellas, wood carvings, henna tattoos and jewelry.

On a scale of 1-10 as far as aggressiveness, I would give the beach vendors in town a five. If you show no interest in anything, they will usually move on. Those that buy something are targeted by every vendor around, like bees to honey.

Some of the indigenous people travel a large distance every day to sell their hand-made bracelets and anklets. Andres has been coming to

Sayulita for over a decade and he walks the main beach everyday selling a variety of colorful beaded bracelets.

Most of the beachfront restaurants allow the vendors to sell to their customers. This is normal and even if you are a big shopper, you will become fluent in saying 'no gracias.'

I make it a point when at El Costenos if I see Andres walking the beach, I will offer to buy him a beer. Just thinking of walking the beach every day for over a decade makes me thirsty!

The main beach also plays host to movie night every once in awhile between Don Pedros and El Costenos. They show retro beach themed movies projected on a screen, such as 'Point Break' and serve beer and other beverages.

The North Beach

Just past the river, on the north end is the mellow north beach. If you just want to lie out and get some sun, this is the area for you. Located away from the bustle of the main beach, the tempo on the north end is relaxed.

A few places have umbrellas and lounges set out, but nothing overwhelming. You can still easily find a spot to throw out the towel and umbrella.

Feel free to bring coolers and even portable barbecues for the day. You will find people selling **shrimp on a stick** walking the beach on this end, as well as a few other vendors. Alcohol is allowed on the beach and all that is asked is that you take out what you brought in.

You will also find the **turtle egg** sanctuary on the north end. Located just past La Terrazolas, they have a protected area where the turtles will come and lay their eggs. It is highly illegal to remove turtle eggs from here.

La Terrazolas is a cool place to hang out and have a drink or some food. They make margaritas with fresh lime juice and put out nice wooden lounge chairs with umbrellas. It is really nice to sit in these and take in the **sunset** over a cocktail.

On weekends you may catch large rave type parties on the beach. These are usually just on the north side of the river and can go well into the morning.

On the very far end of the north beach is a vacation rental. To the right of that is a jungle trail which runs all the way to the **hidden beach.** This can only be accessed by boat or the trail and is almost always un-crowded. It is a little bit of a hike, so bring items that you are comfortable carrying a distance.

Years ago, there was a man who was robbing unsuspecting tourists on the trail. This went on for a few months until people finally got fed up and contacted the governor. The man was arrested shortly after that and no new incidents have occurred since.

Playa Los Muertos

Passing the Villa Amor resort on the south end, you will follow a dirt road which heads up a small hill. Once you are on top of the hill, to the left is the Los Muertos graveyard. This is still used to this day and is sacred to the locals.

At the bottom of the hill, you reach a beach know as **Playa Los Muertos.** This beach is popular with almost everyone and spans about 150 yards from end to end.

No restaurants or facilities exist here, so aside from a few vendors selling fruit, drinks and other light fare, you must bring in everything you want for your stay.

The water is relatively shallow for a good 20 yards off shore, making it perfect for people who want to get wet, but not necessarily to swim.

Being set in a cove, the water is almost always calm here. You can sometimes see people with snorkels and spear-guns swimming around the rocks fishing.

There are no lifeguards on duty, so being alert is important. Police patrol the often frequently looking for anything out of the ordinary. The public schools occasionally have **field trips** to Los Muertos for their students.

Playa Los Muertos can be accessed by foot, automobile and golf car. During weekends in the winter it is not unusual to have this beach packed with people from all over.

Unfortunately there currently are not any bathrooms on the beach or in the vicinity. It is best to use the facilities in town right before you set off for Los Muertos. Some people choose to wade out into the shallow water to take a piss, but it is also only a 10 minute walk back to town in case of emergency.

Surfing and SUP

25 years ago, I first came to Sayulita. Hung-over, I caught an overcrowded bus from Puerto Vallarta one morning. It let me off at the junction of the main highway and the road into Sayulita. At that time there were not any direct buses into town.

The road was dirt and it was fucking hot, so I walked toward the water. Scattered along the beach were trailers and dotting the water surfers. Only one restaurant with about four tables existed on the beach at the time. They served whatever they caught that day and luckily had beer. That restaurant is now much larger but still called El Costenos.

Surfing put Sayulita on the proverbial map. The break is relatively small and is perfect for beginners and intermediates. As this is not much of a challenge for more advance surfers, you can occasionally see people surfing with their dogs or doing headstands on their boards.

The main beach hosts the main break. Along with the umbrellas on the beach you will find tents set up advertising surf instruction for beginners.

You will also find quite a number of **surf instructors** in the town of Sayulita. Some of them even guarantee that you will stand up during the lesson. Sit back and check out the instructors at work if you are curious to see which is right for you.

Knowing how to surf and teaching someone how to surf believe it or not are very far apart. It is like people coming and feeling they are qualified to teach English, simply because they can speak the language. I recommend not walking but running away when approached by one of these.

There have been visitors coming and surfing Sayulita for over three decades, so there isn't a big *'local's only'* attitude. That being said, you may come across a little of it, especially if you are a beginner and have no clue about surfing etiquette.

All of the local surfers know each other, so when picking an instructor, look for someone who is a local. This will help also when paddling out for the first time on your own. It may be helpful to remember the name of your instructor if you come across any issues out in the water.

If you have the basics down and are over the Sayulita break, a few companies have emerged to take people to some of the nearby breaks. **Burroughs** is a very popular intermediate break, located about 2 miles from Punta de Mita. It is accessed only by foot, so if you drive from Mita toward La Cruz, you will see cars lined up on the side of the main road.

There is no such thing as a secret surf break, just some people know where they are more than others. For this reason, take one of the guided surf trips. It will save you a lot of time and if you just want to get some surfing in and not much time to do it, these are well worth it.

Surfboards are also available for **rent** from many different places in town. They have long boards, short boards and body boards available for rent either by the hour, day or week. Feel free to negotiate a fair rate with them, as there is a lot of competition.

In the past decade there is a huge rise in what is known as stand up paddling, or **SUP**. For those that aren't familiar with this, you have an extra large surfboard and a double-sided oar. Once you get up you stay up and gently paddle to a small wave.

There are also instructors for this now, although not as many as with surfing. Some people don't even do this to catch waves, but just like kayaking, go out and paddle around past the surfers waiting for a solid ride.

La Punta Sayulita, a high-end developer in town, for years has been host to an SUP invitational weekend during the high season. This attracts people from all over and is a lot of fun to watch. The best spot to be a spectator is from one of the beach restaurants on the main beach.

Nightlife

"Nothing ever good happens after midnight." That statement holds true in Sayulita. In fact the majority of places shut down around 10pm. That being said, there are a few bars that stay open well into the evening. These are situated around the main plaza, just follow the music.

One of the most popular spots is **Don Pato's** bar. It is located on the upper level across from the plaza on the south side and has a sweet view of the plaza. They have a nice open air lounge style atmosphere and you can sometimes find live music in the evenings.

Known as **The Gringo Bar** to locals, the spot on the north-east corner, across from the plaza is once again in operation. This bar is located on the street level and has a DJ most Friday and Saturday evenings.

On Monday evenings during the high-season, Don Pedros hosts a **Cuban Night**. A door fee is charged and they have a live band and Cuban style dancing on the main restaurant floor.

Across the plaza, upstairs and next to Choc Banana, is **El Tigre**. This is the same name as the surf school and they are affiliated. They have a full bar and a juke-box.

On some nights you find people throwing **beach parties** on the main beach at night. Sometimes they can be almost like raves in the sand. These can be usually be found on the north end, just past the river. The crowds are usually friendly and relaxed.

Fighting is heavily frowned upon in Sayulita and unlike the common bar fight up north, there's a good chance if you are involved in a fight, you will be taken to jail.

At one of the bars that attract locals, a waiter got into an argument with one of the local electricians. It escalated and the waiter ended up smashing a bottle over the other man's head. This created a huge cut and blood gushed out of the wound.

The man was taken to San Pancho, where he got stitches. When asked if he was going to pursue charges, the man declined saying it was nothing.

Medical

In town you will find an assortment of **pharmacies** which carry a variety of remedies that you can self administer. These can be anything from crèmes and ointments, to prescription strength medication.

Unlike up north and even in other parts of Mexico, a prescription is not required to get certain medication in Sayulita. One can get generic Adderall, Valium, Xanax, Zoloft and Tylenol three, just by asking for it. Please be aware that it is illegal to have prescription meds without a prescription, even in Mexico.

Located in the OXXO plaza off of the main highway is **Sayulita Urgent Care**. They actually cater to North Americans and other visitors. English is usually spoken. They are equipped to handle emergencies for a short period of time.

For emergencies, the nearest hospital is in San Pancho/ San Francisco, about 20 minutes from Sayulita. This is a full service facility and able to handle a variety of emergencies.

A young woman was mountain biking and suffered a knee injury. When she arrived at the hospital, they recommended cutting her leg off at the knee. Looking for a second opinion, she traveled to the U.S.

Once there she entered a medical facility and was given a prescription for anti-inflammatory medication and pain killers. I'm not here to bash on Mexico's medical system, but sometimes if possible, it pays to get a second opinion.

For the people of Sayulita, there is a national health care system known as **El Centro de Salud**. With a staff of usually under three people, including a doctor, people can get to see a physician and receive treatment for problems like infections, ear aches, intestinal problems, etc...

They are limited in what they can do, but really come through if you become ill. When the dengue breakout of 2012 hit Sayulita, the Salud was there for many of the residents of town.

Running solely off of donations, they do not actually charge for their services. It is encouraged if you get treatment for something and you are financially able, to give a donation.

Drugs

If you walk the main beach, more often than not you will be approached by a vendor and offered **marijuana**. Please be aware that in Mexico, marijuana is still illegal.

The product down here is very low quality and sometimes is referred to as a, 'headache in a bag.' Compare this to the variety of green bud that is available in Washington, Colorado and British Columbia and you will be disappointed.

For those that need to smoke, recently a traveler picked up a baggie of an ounce of marijuana for $2000 pesos. Unlike other parts of the country, law enforcement in Sayulita doesn't seem to care much about the casual traveler and small amounts of weed.

A couple of years ago, a young charismatic man came to town to make and sell donuts. A very likeable individual, he walked the streets of Sayulita, wearing a cook's uniform verbally advertising his donuts as the best in the world. Most of the donuts were straight, but he kept some that were infused with marijuana.

Not concerned about the police, he would constantly say that they were his homies. One day, one of the commandantes' called him into his office. He showed him photos that were taken of him selling his magic donuts.

Blowing it off, the young man still continued going about, selling his donuts both loaded and unloaded. A few days later he was nowhere to be found. He usually had a larger than life presence and soon it was obvious that something had happened.

A few weeks later the word in town was that he was picked up and in the main jail in Tepic awaiting deportation to the United States. To this day he unfortunately has never returned to Sayulita.

Pharmacies are all over Sayulita. Here you can find a variety of generic **prescription drugs** available over the counter. It is best to have prior experience with what you are asking for, as there are not any doctors to guide you.

Generic **valium** and **xanax** are available at around 20 pills for $400 pesos. If you want Tylenol with **codeine**, it will run you around $1500- $2000 pesos for 30 capsules. Believe it or not, vicodin, hydrocodone and percoset are not available, even with a prescription.

A few years ago, there was a self-proclaimed nurse that walked around town with a stethoscope around her neck. Originally from North America, she would seek out individuals, more specific, single, older men who suffer from medical conditions.

I knew one her victims who bought into her Florence Nightingale story. She would go into the pharmacies and buy large quantities of liquid valium. Not having any medical knowledge, he would allow her to inject him with 'medicine'.

Truly unbelievable, the man would be completely out of it and pay her for her services even though he had no idea what she was doing. One day she hooks up with a resident in town under the guise of being his personal physician. About a year after that, she was found dead on the side of a river. To this day it is unclear who killed her, but the reason why is pretty obvious.

Mixing prescription drugs with alcohol is a recipe for disaster. In Sayulita it is very easy to not think about this until it is too late. No one is here to tell you what to do and what not to. This includes the police and people in town. The reality is that no one cares, so you are left with yourself to decide right from wrong.

A young lady arrived in Sayulita and decided she was going to deal ecstasy and cocaine. When asked about the product, she claimed she was receiving it from Canada and it was of the highest quality. To avoid problems, she had a plan to move to a different area every couple of days, so as not to bring attention to herself. At the point of this writing she is either on her way to a popular area in South America, in jail or dead.

Harder drugs like cocaine, methamphetamine and heroin can also be obtained in Sayulita, although a little harder to find and definitely something to stay away from. It is not recommended to get involved with drugs in Sayulita, but they exist nonetheless.

With a general laissez-faire attitude surrounding drugs in Sayulita, about three years ago there was a buzz about a stand that had just opened up on the other side of the river.

Apparently someone thought it would be profitable to set up a drug table, selling marijuana, cocaine and pretty much anything. Many in the town just shook their heads and soon after it was quickly removed.

Jail

When someone is arrested, the police will handcuff the person ot the roll-bar in the back of their truck. One of the officers will sit in the truck bed with the person or people. It is not unusual to see multiple people in the back of a truck.

Those that are arrested in Sayulita are taken to either the recently constructed jail in Bucerias or the main jail in Valle. Valle is located about 40 minutes from Sayulita.

Processing is done at the jail and you are searched, fingerprinted and put into a general, open-air area with other people. This is where drinks, fighters and people who commit general offenses are taken.

This is basically a holding facility and if you are in for being drunk or fighting, you can usually pay a fine after about 12-24 hours after entering the facility.

During your time there they have a roll-call that is given about every hour. A list of the names of current detainees is read off and when you hear your name, you say, "presente."

A plastic jug of water is passed around and there is one toilet for the entire area. Generally hot, crowded and uncomfortable, the time will go by very slow. This isn't the community style, Mel Gibson jail from the movies and your biggest issue will be passing the time.

Your personal belongings will be returned to you upon release. The police will not steal your money if you have any. In the other sections of the jail facility are sections for women and those who are awaiting transportation to another facility.

Sports

Aside from surfing, there are other sporting activities in Sayulita. During the summer and winter, the Sayulita Jaibos are a **baseball** team made up of locals.

They are a semi-professional team in a league that plays other towns throughout the state. This team has been in Sayulita for decades. Players are paid a minimal amount, with the pitchers receiving the highest amount.

Travelling by bus, they play teams as far away as 5 hours one way. Unlike their minor league counterparts up north, the players travel by bus, play the game and then return, sometimes travelling most of the evening.

Years ago, this used to be a beer league. In the past few years it has gained the respect of people who pay a minor fee to enter the ball field, which runs along the river at the beginning of downtown.

Beer and food are sold inside the ballpark by local vendors. There is also a raffle that is held. People walk around with notebooks informing the crowd of the prize and cost. You can pay anywhere from 15-40 pesos and choose a number on a sheet of paper. If your number is called, you win the prize on that paper. Usually it is a case of beer, bottle of liquor or some other item.

The players wear uniforms and have skills. When someone asked me at a game last year, what stage of the American minor leagues I would class them in, I told them probably single A.

Spectators can enter through two different entrances. The one that runs along the 3rd base line and the river is generally for the home fans. There are bleachers that are set up just past the infield, but during the day the sun beats heavily down on them.

The main entrance is located just before the bridge and has access to the covered, permanent bleachers. There isn't really a set home and visitors side, so if you want to have a seat in the shade, this is the entrance to use. No access is permitted from one side to the other through the field of play.

As of last season, the team consisted of largely local Sayulita people. Most have businesses in town and all are Mexican. I have never seen a North American playing for the Jaibos.

A big tradition with the people of Sayulita is the **cockfights**. They have an area set up just across from the bull ring and people from all over come to enter their rooster.

To enter a rooster, they must fall into a certain weight category. A fee is paid and a cash purse is up for grabs. The amounts vary depending on the schedule that day.

While in town, you may see people with a hand wrapped up in a bandage. This is from the cockfights. You see, long razors are attached to the feet of the birds and every once in awhile an accident happens and someone gets their hand sliced.

The cost for a spectator to enter is usually around $100 pesos. They serve beer and other refreshments inside and have bleacher type seating. Gambling is not only allowed, it is encouraged on the fights and the crowd really gets into it.

Just like a lot of things in Sayulita, if you don't like it, don't go see it. The last thing people care about is a foreigner's opinion on something.

Right across from the cockfighting area is the bull ring. This is used on occasion to host roping contests and general **rodeos**. At times they also have live banda groups performing.

Attending one of these events is a fun experience and most of the people get dressed up. Vendors walk the stone steps of the bull ring selling beer, potato chips with hot sauce and just about anything that will sell. These events start late and can go into the wee hours of the morning most of the time.

For those that are more comfortable watching **sports on television**, there are a couple of solid places. The first is _Alleya's Nachos and Wings._ The owner Josue speaks both English and Spanish and for major evening events, he has a big-screen set up across the street from his restaurant.

For the NFL playoffs he did a Texas style barbecue for a minimal price. This is a very fun and relaxed place to watch a game. The prices are also very reasonable.

Another great place to watch a game is Don Pedro's. The staff are solid and you are right on the water, so usually a nice breeze flows through the restaurant.

There are 2 flat screen TVs at the bar and another one in the main seating area of the restaurant. During the Super Bowl they have a traditional football pool you can buy into.

Watching soccer is the main sport for people in town and there are two teams that the majority of people root for. The first is **Chivas** of Guadalajara. With the close proximity to the city, it is only logical for this to be a favorite.

The other team is **Club America.** They are based out of Mexico City, so a good sized following is in Sayulita. It really gets interesting when the two teams play each other and then you really see the genuine passion of the people.

Vendors

The number of people selling their wares has increased tremendously and goes well beyond just the beach. In recent years, numerous vendors have set up along the streets of Sayulita.

Huichal people have tables set up in the plaza right in front of Choco-Banana restaurant. Their inventory consists hand-made jewelry and other colorful items. They can be observed actually creating the items during the course of the day.

A tradition on Sundays is the **flea-market** or *tianguis* located on the block of Calle Gaviotas between the OXXO and the community center. This is often crowded and just a small walking area separate the tarp covered sections. Here people shop for shoes, shirts and other clothing items.

The hours of the flea-market are around 9am to about 2pm. The vendors arrive in the early morning to begin setting up their stands for the day. Fresh fruit is often for sale here, with the booth across from the community center. Pieces of fresh mango, papaya, and various types of melon are cut and placed in a plastic container with a fork so you can eat on the go.

During the high season there is an **Organic Market** that invites people who have organic products to come and sell them. This is located along the river and all the way to the beach, just down from Duende's Tacos and Pizza Ron.

You will find **Sidewalk Vendors** with their individual tables on some of the side streets heading to the beach. The block of Gaviotas from the community center to Captain Pablo's restaurant is one that allows the various vendors to set up tables on the side of the street and sell items, usually some type of jewelry.

Usually walking around Sayulita, you will see people carrying a variety of items for sale. Individuals stroll along displaying their items for sale.

Some of the things available from the **Strolling Vendors** include hammocks, belts, portable music players and usb's, a variety of DVDs' and wallets.

Their prices are reasonable and you can buy five DVDs' for $100 pesos. A belt will cost around one-hundred and fifty. Although they don't have a specific location of time, you can usually find them out during the height of the day.

Dogs

Dogs are a big part of Sayulita and literally everywhere in town. From strays to pets, you can see them on the streets and the beach all hours of the day.

Sayulita Animals is the child of Swiss born Sayulita resident Sara Carmen Briner. The pioneer in town when it comes to helping the dog population, her organization survives on donations.

Located on the dirt road separating the Punta Mita highway and the main road into town, Sayulita Animals is the only agency in town responsible for the spaying and neutering of dogs.

The general attitude of the Mexican people towards dogs is far from different than that of North Americans. You may come across a dog that is unkempt and frail. Don't just assume that this a homeless animal. It could very well be a family's pet and actually has a home in Sayulita.

A couple who migrated to Sayulita had a child. When the child was a little older, it wanted a puppy. This is like most children, however when this puppy became a dog. The man drove towards Tepic and let it out of the car abandoning it. The man is American and the woman is from Guadalajara.

It is not uncommon to see dogs in some restaurants in town. Although not all restaurants in town allow dogs, there are still some that welcome the furry friends.

There are dogs that are up for adoption and it is common for a foreigner to adopt a dog and take it home with them. In order to bring a dog back with you, you must have all the vaccinations current and verified. Sayulita Animals can help you with this process and Sarah is familiar with the vaccination requirements for different countries.

A young couple from the state of Washington visited Sayulita and rented a home on 'Gringo Hill.' When they arrived a scruffy dog was waiting for them. They fed it and generally took care it during their stay, the dog even sleeping on the property.

The day before they were to go home they were encouraged to inquire about the dog. It turned out the dog belonged to a family who lived down the street from the vacation home they were in.

Internet, Cell Phones and Mail

Sayluita is dialed in when it comes to the **internet**. Many of the restaurants in town provide free internet access to their customers. Though most are open seasonally, both Choco Banana and Don Pedro's are year-round.

You will find that most restaurants will provide electrical outlets for your devices if you if ask. Signal strength for each place depends on your devices proximity to the modem. In Choco Banana, the modem is located just inside the kitchen window. Don Pedro's has theirs in the middle of the bar.

One of my personal favorites is **Don Juan's** restaurant, next to the La China market and just off the Punta Mita road. They have a nice open air atmosphere and a relaxing attitude. All of my published books and short stories were finished here.

Luna-Net is located just off the main plaza and across from the Gringo bar. This has computers and internet and is charged by the duration of use. Fabian, the owner also does comprehensive computer repair work here.

On the road after the bridge is another internet facility. It is connected with the produce market next door. This is open all year, but unfortunately does not provide air-conditioning.

Like everywhere in the world, **cell phones** are in Sayulita as well. The main service provider is **TelCel**, owned by one of the richest men in the world, Carlos Slim.

It seems that AT&T works together with TelCel. Before leaving for Mexico, check with your service provider on a plan that works while you are in Sayulita. I know that AT&T offers a full coverage, non roaming plan for a fee of around $40.00 USD for a week.

Something that is baffling is that in Sayulita, **mail service** is almost non-existent. **DHL** is probably your best bet if you want to receive something from home.

A few years ago, a place called Sayulita Sun offered mail boxes to the people of Sayulita for a yearly fee. This went out of business and nothing has since replaced it.

Occasionally a mail carrier from Bucerias will come to town delivering mail. This is ridiculous, as they usually have no idea where they are going and mail ends up everywhere. If you are expecting something important, first make sure you have an actual address and second send it DHL with a tracking number.

Locals

For over 30 years, the people of Sayulita have seen a steady stream of foreigners come to town. I' m not talking about the all knowing foreigner that was here before the dawn of time according to them, but actual Mexican people.

The general attitude is one of acceptance. People can easily mingle with the locals. You will find if you talk to people that many of them are related to each other in one way or another.

The owner of El Espresso café was a local woman Jessica, who sadly passed away last year in an automobile accident. She had one of largest attended memorial services that has ever been witnessed in Sayulita.

Something that amazes me to this day is the belief that buying property in Sayulita makes you a local. It really doesn't matter how much money you have, or how large of a property you own, if you come from another place, you are not a local. This includes myself and I don not try to pass myself off as a local, though I am both Mexican and American.

A year ago, people were walking down one of the dirt roads to the beach. A foreigner was sweeping the dusty street and when asked why he was doing it, he said he was leading by example for the local people.

Standing around, drinking beer was a small group of young men. They were looking over and laughing at this guy. Now that is a solid example.

In Sayulita there is a group of local people who are known as the **Ejido**. They have a building on Avenida Revolucion, just off of Gaviotas. Although of little importance to visitors, they occasionally throw parties that go well into the night with live music and free beer.

An elected official known as the **Juez** basically serves as a mediator in basic disputes by locals. An example of this would be if a neighbor's dog is shitting on their property, the owner might go the Juez with the problem.

In Sayulita a very nice man named Don Chuey is currently the Juez. He used to run the *loncheria* or cafeteria at the Public Junior High School. You can now find him selling beer at the Sayulita baseball games during the season.

Side Trips

If you have some time to spend, you will find that Sayulita becomes routine after a few days. There are towns and cities with their individual personalities less than three hours away.

There is a rental car agency located right in town across from the 'Drunk Tree.' Here you can rent different sized cars, just as you would at the airport.

Just about a 20 minute ride is the town of **Punta de Mita**. This is where you will find the exclusive **Punta Mita** resort, home of two Jack Nicklaus signature golf courses. This is not accessible to the general public.

The surrounding town is basically a row of **waterfront restaurants** and a hotel. Most of them offer a variety of fresh seafood in an open air setting. Generally open for lunch and dinner you can drive down along the main road and notice the waiters standing outside promoting their individual spots. This is a solid destination for lunch or dinner on the beach.

The **Marietta Islands** are a very cool set of islands just off the coast of Punta de Mita. In town you can rent a fishing charter that will take you to the famous **hidden beach**.

The hidden beach in all actuality is really not that hidden and you will notice many boats sitting just off the shore of the island. People swim with life jackets through a watery cave that opens up to a nice beach inside the island.

Fishermen are located all over the area and even when you drive into the town. They generally offer similar trips that range from $1500 to $3000 pesos for a fishing trip to the Marietta's.

The fishermen use what are called **Pangas.** These are skiff-style boats with an outboard motor. Beers, waters and snacks are usually provided by the guide, but ask to be sure.

Amazingly, to get from Sayulita to Punta de Mita you must drive yourself of take a taxi. To this day, there still are not any buses that travel directly between the two places.

You will find two **cantinas** in town. The first is located off the main highway leading into Punta de Mita. It is pretty casual and depending on the season, has a few women working.

The second cantina is located at the far end of restaurant row. This is pretty sketchy and has a few transvestites working on and off. The immediate area smells like shit, literally as a waste treatment facility is about 50 yards away.

Located about 45 minutes north is the authentic Mexican beach town called **Rincon de Guyabitos**. This can be reached by taking a bus labeled Tepic across the main highway.

The bus is air-conditioned and will take you to the town of La Penita, which is just 5 minutes from Guyabitos. You can jump in a taxi from here to take you into the heart of downtown.

Guayabitos is basically made up of a single road that runs through the center of town and the main beach. The tourism here is generally made up of Mexican people visiting from other states and areas in the country.

A variety of restaurants are located on the main street and on the beach. The hotels are built to host families of various sizes. There is all-inclusive hotel called **DeCameron** in Guayabitos located at the very end of town.

If you decide to take a day trip here, you will want to hit the beach. Often crowded, you will immediately see a difference between Sayulita and Guayabitos.

You will see a larger number of vendors on the beach, selling fish and **shrimp on a stick**, fresh fruit and blow up toys. You will also see people selling little plastic figures flying in the air with parachutes similar to flying a kite.

They don't have the restaurant owned chairs and umbrellas on the beach. The umbrellas you see are brought in by the visitors, as well as a cooler generally.

If you take a walk along the edge of the water you will see a large amount of children playing in the water. They float around on the blow up toys and the general attitude is carefree.

Surfing is not something you will find in Guayabitos, but located about a mile off shore is a small island. A party boat cruises around this and you will find people selling tickets for it on the beach.

By far the most popular side trip from Sayulita is to **Puerto Vallarta**. A 45 minute ride will get you down to the Malecon, or boardwalk.

If you are taking a bus, it can be picked up at the entrance to the main part of town. It runs every 20 minutes beginning on the hour. The **last bus leaves Vallarta around 10:30pm** or so, depending on where you are in, so be aware of the time, as the first bus from P.V. leaves at 6 am. The one-way fare on the Compostella bus is **30 pesos**.

If you haven't been here, it really is a pretty fun place to visit. They have gourmet restaurants, popping nightclubs and lots of shopping. I'm not going to go into boring detail about the different places, as you can find that anywhere.

What I will tell you are the places that you will find here and not in Sayulita. The first things are the **casinos**. There are two located in or around the Gallerias shopping mall, across from where the Cruise Ships dock. They are both relatively the same, so I will just describe one in this guide.

The casino inside the mall has everything you will find in places where gambling is legal. Table games like **roulette** and **blackjack**, with actual dealers are in the back area. This is also the designated smoking area as it is not permitted in the general area.

The main area has video slot machines. A girl walks around selling tickets with various amounts on them. You will have a code on the ticket with the amount purchased. To use it, go to the machine you want to play and type in the code from the ticket. The amount will automatically be transferred to the machine. When you cash out, the funds will automatically be transferred to that ticket.

In the center of the casino, there is a circular bar, with chairs along the edge of it. They have servers waking around, but this can be hit or miss. Beers are really inexpensive in here and a Pacifico will run you around 15 pesos. They also serve decent and relatively inexpensive food

A **sports book** is located just to the side of the entrance. Here you can watch 10 screens of various sports, as well as 8 screens of live horseracing. They usually have between 1 to 2 cashiers working at a time. You can bet on any sporting event in a variety of ways, including a straight bet, parlay or teaser.

For the best mojitos in town, head to the **Cuban Bar** located on the malecon. Here you can see the names of different people who have visited written on the walls.

A popular place for the ambience, view and **dollar beer** is the Cheeky Monkey. The entrance is located just off the malecon, but the seating overlooks the ocean. They have a beachfront sister restaurant called the Sea Monkey, located in old town. One of the highlights here are the huge onion rings.

Located along the river is a market that is pretty cool. A variety of vendors sell their items here and the original **River Café** is also located here. This is a nice place to come for dinner or a drink after a day of shopping. There is a cool footbridge going from the market into old town.

The **zoo** is great place to go and is just beyond the tunnel. They have a variety of different wildlife here and it is really well maintained. They charge a minimal entrance fee and this is accessed by car.

Located in the Fluvial area of Puerto Vallarta is **Costco**. It is exactly like the Costco's in the United States and you can everything in bulk here. They have the quarter pound, all beef hot dog and soda combo here as well. All beef hot dogs are starting to pop up in more places in Mexico, but Costco still has the best in the area.

If you want actual, fresh **Cuban cigars**, head to the end of the malecon and walk towards the Burger King, just off the plaza. Take a right down the road and about 2 blocks down you will find the Cuban cigar store. They only carry Cuban cigars which are kept inside a separate humidifier room. This place is open year round and has comfortable leather chairs and air conditioning.

You will find one of the most unique towns about 3 hours east in the mountains. **Talpa** is home to the Virgin of Guadalupe and they have pilgrimages to pay homage to her here.

Churches are the heart and soul of this town, but the church of the virgin is the main draw and a thing of beauty in the **main plaza**. This is the hub of Talpa. People go to church in droves at different times of the day to pay their respects.

In the main plaza you will find children shining shoes and vendors selling toys. There is also the company **Talpa Tours** that offer a variety of tours around the area.

Another tour is a mere 50 pesos per person and you can pick it up behind the church in the main plaza. An open air truck with bench seating leaves during the day about every 45 minutes.

They take you to the various churches and up to the monument at the top of the mountain. The views alone are incredible from up here. The guide just speaks in Spanish during the tour, but it is fun to check everything out anyway if you don't understand.

In the early morning and around sunset, a man and his wife have a cart set up selling hot cinnamon with a choice of **rompope** and/or **raicilla**. Both of these are alcoholic, however the raicilla can be likened to moonshine with high proof.

Both rompope and raicilla are sold everywhere in Talpa. Although this is true, it is definitely not a party town and you will find almost everything closed after 10pm.

On the main street there are a few restaurants that serve breakfast, lunch and dinner. One which just was renovated is directly in front of the main plaza, with open air views of the church of the Virgin.

You will find mostly traditional Mexican food served in Talpa, along with hamburgers. In the evening, carts set up close to the main plaza selling tacos.

Located in the hillside and about a 10 minute walk up the hill is a casual restaurant that is rustic and serves baked potatoes, steaks and other grilled dishes. This offers beautiful views of the plaza and the area.

This is too far to go during the day, so you will most likely be staying here. For the most part, Talpa caters to the people who do the pilgrimage so **hotels** are very basic. Most have showers with hot water and cable TV. The price is also relatively basic at only about $200 pesos per night. You will see a few multi-room hotels with their prices shown outside along the main street within 5 blocks from the plaza.

Guadalajara is the second largest city in Mexico and the capital of Jalisco. I will not spend much time on it, but give some helpful insight to the city for the first time visitor.

To get here, a bus leaves twice a week from Sayulita and will cost about $350 pesos. You can also drive on your own. If you drive you will come across toll roads. The tolls will vary in price usually between $40 and $130 pesos per car. Expect to pay around $500 pesos for the one-way trip.

Beginning just after the city of Compostella, you will have a choice to take the toll road or opt for the free one. If you can, take the toll road, it is two lanes with a speed limit on average of 90 kilometers per hour. Rarely is there traffic here, so you can pretty much open it up.

After one of the toll booths close to Guadalajara there is a **rest area** with a store selling drinks and snacks. You will also see vendors sell pouches of tequila for the road.

The main downtown area is where you will find a variety of hotels. **Hotel Morales** is within walking distance to the main plazas and right across from the park with the horse and buggy tours. They also have valet parking, so just roll up in the busy front entrance area and someone will take care of your car. Parking is disgusting in this city, so this is a huge benefit.

The **horse and buggy tours** are a great way to see the different neighborhoods surrounding the downtown area. Your driver will give a historical narration throughout your tour. Did you know the actual bodies are buried underneath the statues that line one of the streets around the plaza?

The cost for a short, 30 minute tour will be around $350 pesos and the full tour is $500 pesos. This lasts close to an hour and is very comprehensive. I would recommend taking this tour on your first evening in the city to see where you want to go.

You can also book the popular **Tequila Train** at the hotel. It leaves in the mornings, so you must book it the day before travelling. This will take you to the town of tequila, complete with tasting on and off the train.

On practically every block you will find two things **downtown**. The first is a **Chinese food buffet** and the second either a **bookstore** or a **music store** selling instruments.

On the **weekends** there is a huge multi level flea market just down from the main plazas downtown. Here you get everything and I mean everything including a variety of birds and pets.

In the main plaza, the city offers **free Wi-Fi**. They also have electrical outlets in the plaza and fee for people to use to charge their personal electronic devices.

Unfortunately the food choices in and around the main plazas could use some help. Someone once asked, 'How do you screw up eggs?!?!'

Sundays they close the main street during the mid-morning hours to **bicycles**, which is very cool. Unfortunately if you are leaving on Sunday, this could cause a little bit of a challenge.

Something that is a must experience is the area surrounding the **United States Embassy**. The buildings are beautifully constructed and some even have been converted to restaurants.

You will find top notch restaurants from many different countries serving deliciously authentic dishes in this neighborhood. In the evening these draw a culturally diverse crowd from all over the city. A fairly long walk from downtown, you can take either a bus or a taxi to the area for a minimal charge.

Years ago the crime was an issue in Guadalajara, where even downtown after dark it was sketchy to walk around. This has changed for the better. Downtown is relatively safe to walk around and you will see a large police presence here.

Obviously this is a big city and big city problems are here. Use common sense when exploring the area and it is recommended to have someone with you.

Bikes, Boats and ATVs

Renting bikes is something that has gained popularity in Sayulita over recent years. On the north end of town, on Calle Miramar, you will find a young man named Adrian.

A young mountain bike enthusiast named **Adrian** has been involved in riding in Sayulita since a very young age and knows all of the trails from Sayulita to Punta de Mita. He runs a bicycle repair business on Calle Miramar on the north-end of town and can recommend a place to rent bikes and also be hired as a guide as well.

Riding in town is kind of difficult because of the cobblestone streets downtown. For some reason, people think is a smart idea to bike from Sayulita to **San Pancho**. This is incredibly dangerous and should be avoided. Unlike the US and Canada, bicyclists in Mexico in reality are not given the 'right of way.' Traveling on the two-lane highway, with no bike lane and a very limited shoulder most of the way is a recipe for disaster.

Many people choose to ride this route and very nasty accidents have occurred simply because there aren't any bike lanes. Car are travelling sometimes in excess of 80 KMH. They will pass cars on a double yellow and if you are unlucky enough to be riding when a car needs to cut over, chances are you will be in trouble.

The **Punta de Mita highway** is popular with cyclists and has relatively light traffic throughout the day. The route from Sayulita to Punta de Mita is about 15 miles.

A fun way to spend a day is on a **party boat**. There are a couple of options in town but for overall enjoyment, I would recommend **Chica Loca**.

Gil and his father Ali run a solid operation and you won't have any unfortunate surprises with them. They have an office just down from the plaza and next to Ruben's Deli.

The day begins where you board an open air vehicle next to the office early in the morning. This will take you to the La Cruz marina where you will board the Chica Loca catamaran.

This cruise will take you leisurely out to the Marietta Islands where you can swim to the hidden beach and slide off the catamaran's waterslide into the refreshing water.

During the trip, deckhands walk around serving drinks and snacks. Party music is played throughout the day and the staff also throw out some trolling lines. If they catch fish during the trip, it will be prepared and served as *ceviche* to the guests.

Chica Loca is all-inclusive and includes all of your drinks and food throughout your day. The food is catered by Ruben's Deli that has the best sandwiches in Sayulita.

If you are interested in **zip-lines** and **ATVs**, then you will want to pay a visit to Rancho Mi Chaparrita. This is the premiere Adventure Tour Company of Sayulita.

Local businessman Luis Verdin has built a solid company with the main office located on the street right across from the sports field. They offer customers guided ATV tours down the Punta Mita highway, where you will follow a staff member in a **four-seat Razor 4 ATV**. They provide everyone with helmets and bandannas for the dust.

Quads have become a thing of the past in Sayulita when it comes to tourists, though you will still see individuals riding them around town. Something that is unique is that motorized recreational vehicles are not allowed in the water and this includes all jet skis and wave runners.

A group of friends visiting Sayulita decided to rent one of the fishing charters. They brought along with them a drone and asked if they could fly off the neighboring beach. The fishing guide had never seen anything like it, so he said, "why not?" After pulling up to the beach one of the friends began flying it.

As they left the beach, they were met in the ocean by Federales. They informed the group that it was illegal and prohibited to fly any drones in the area. The tourists explained that they had no idea it was *against the law. In the end, the owner of the fishing charter was issued a $300 USD fine.*

Luis Verdin's large, mountainous property is located just down the Punta Mita highway. This is home to Sayulita's only **zip-line** facility and recreation area with a swimming pool.

Guest are brought to the facility in an open-air vehicle from the **Rancho Mi Chaparrita** office in town. The group is then fitted with harnesses, helmets and gloves. The staff here are very personal and make the whole experience a lot of fun.

After finishing up zip-lining, you can head to the pool area and go **swimming in the pool**. There are tables and chairs set up around, but unfortunately no food is served. They do serve sodas and on occasion alcohol, but it is smart to bring your own supplies. They do have refrigerators where you can ask to store your food and drinks.

Festivals and Holidays

Sayulita comes alive when it comes to Holidays and Festivals. I will not go into the stories and history of the different holidays, but only let you know how they pertain to Sayulita.

September 16th marks Mexico's **Independence Day.** This is similar to the 4th of July in the United States. In Sayluita, this is the time for a parade. All of the schools in town participate in a colorful parade through town. This begins around 9am and usually starts on the north end and goes all the way to the plaza.

At the plaza, cowboys and their dancing horses can be seen providing entertainment for the crowd. Often times they have live, local entertainment performing on a stage in the main plaza.

The day which celebrates Pancho Villa and Emiliano Zapata is on **November 20th**. This is known as **Revolution Day** and it is celebrated in Sayulita. You can see children dressed up as revolutionaries taking part in the morning parade through town.

At the plaza the horsemen and live music provide entertainment for the crowd.

For a week leading up to **December 12th**, the **Lady of Guadalupe** festival occurs. This is celebrated with loud explosions which can be heard throughout the town beginning at 5am.

This all culminates on the final day in the plaza, where a large fireworks display is set up. In the evening, '**bulls**' made up of hundreds of fireworks are carried through the plaza.

The young men holding the bulls run around chasing and being chased by revelers. You should be cautious when 'running with the bulls' in Sayulita, as very often firework related accidents occur and the celebration continues.

Sayulita Days come during the month of February and this is when the carnival comes to town. Usually set up in and around the sports field, people can participate in a variety of games, like throwing rocks at bottles to win beers. They have a number of low-level amusement park rides that open up in the evening. The admission is free to get in the sports field

There is also an evening rodeo that takes place one evening in the bull ring located at the beginning of town. It is a unique, Mexican experience to enter and you can see many of the Sayulita locals dressed up and in attendance.

Halloween is a fun day of the year when children can dress up as their favorite characters and go trick or treating. In Sayulita, this day has grown throughout the years with children gathering at the plaza and candy being given out.

The days after Halloween mark the **Day of the Dead**. This has absolutely nothing to do with Halloween and is to remember loved ones that have passed on. During the week leading up to November 1-2, people decorate the main plaza with personal altars.

The altars are often adorned with flowers, candles and a picture of the deceased. '*Pan de Muerto*' is sold in stores and also by vendors in town during this time. The tradition is to share the round bread with close friends and family. There are multiple plastic '*babies*' hidden within the bread and those people that get the 'babies', must cook tamales for the rest of the group.

Donating

Many tourists visiting Sayulita want to try and assist the local community by giving donations. Many groups and institutions exist largely because of the generous donations given.

Unfortunately greed and flat out lies are used by some in order to raise donations. Money is the main goal of these institutions and not helping the local community.

In Sayulita both **public schools** and a **private school** exist. There is a public elementary located on the north end of town and a public junior high school just off the Punta Mita highway. There are also a handful of public kindergartens in town.

Over the years people and even organizations in Sayulita have donated money to different public schools in order to better the institutions. This money has more than often than not, been stolen by the principles in charge of the schools.

The children who attend public schools must provide their own uniforms and school supplies. To help them, it is strongly encouraged <u>not</u> to donate money, but to donate supplies.

When the principle of the public junior high wanted to complete a project on the grounds of the school, she asked for money. She asked using the poor state of education in Sayulita line as the excuse. When volunteers offered to build what was needed the principle outright refused their help. The project to this day still remains unfinished.

The private school in Sayulita is known as **Costa Verde**. They claim this is a non-profit, which is a blatant lie. In hiring one of their recent teacher hires, the main focus of the interview wasn't educational experience, but experience with fundraisers.

Costa Verde charges students a large annual tuition and they claim that they have a large number of 'scholarship' students. If you ask the ratio of scholarship students to tuition students, you will not get a straight answer. If you are in the dark, this institution was founded and is run by high salaried North Americans for obvious profit.

For all the stray and abused dogs in Sayulita, there is hope. Sara Carmen Briner runs **Sayluita Animals**. This is a true non-profit organization with a volunteer veterinarian and nurse.

They are responsible for a large amount the spaying and neutering of animals in Sayulita and rely heavily on donations. They have an office located on the dirt road between Calle Revolucion and the Punta Mita highway at the beginning of town, where the police and fire stations are currently located.

All of the recycling in Sayulita originated as the brain child of Tracy Willis, the owner of Choco Banana restaurant. She also founded **Sayulimpia**, a group that is in charge of keeping Sayulita clean and recycling.

Their **recycling facility** and dump is located just off the Punta Mita highway towards the beginning of town. This is where plastic, glass and cardboard are separated, as well as general trash. They recently erected a fence around the area, as the sight of the dump along the highway esthetically unappealing.

Placed around town you can still find metal trash bins scattered throught. These are mounted on a stand and off the ground to keep them away from animals. Unfortunately people have stolen many of them that were supplied by Tracy Willis personally.

During the year, Tracy Willis organizes a river clean up. This brings **volunteers** and often students together to clean the river from San Ignacio and through the town down to the beach. This also includes the river that empties on the side of Don Pedros and runs behind the Iguana Tree.

For those that are interested in **volunteering**, please contact Tracy Willis. She can be found almost every day at Choco Banana restaurant just off of the plaza.